INTERIOR PORTRAITS

INTERIOR PORTRAITS

A CALIFORNIA DESIGN PILGRIMAGE

PORTRAITS

AT HOME WITH CULTURAL PIONEERS AND CREATIVE MAVERICKS

LESLIE WILLIAMSON

RIZZOLI
NEW YORK

New York Paris London Milan

CONTENTS

I am a homebody. There is nothing I like to do more than walk through my front door at the end of a long day and close it behind me. At home, I am embraced by a little world of my own creation, surrounded by the things that I love, need, want, and find beautiful. That is what our homes are, after all—our own personal worlds that we have made for ourselves.

Over the past decade, I have traveled around the world photographing the homes of other people (it is such a privilege to do what I love that I pinch myself regularly at my good fortune). Some may see my work as "interiors photography" but I have always seen it as a form of portraiture. Don't get me wrong, I love a good interior, but for my books, I have deliberately sought out a very select group of people whose homes are, in essence, the embodiment of who they are and what they do: it's home as a portrait of self. And as a group, the people in my books became my path to understanding a larger idea that I wanted to explore. For a long time, I did not readily discuss the depth of what I see in other people's homes, nor my unorthodox way of delving into ideas. It felt very hard to explain in words since so much of it is wholly intuitive. Yet after the successes of my first two books, which explored modernism through the homes of its creators, I felt more confident—emboldened even—that my approach was more universal than I had ever dared imagine. So I pondered what subject would be next and made list after list of possibilities. And of the many ideas I had, I am still surprised that the subject that called me the loudest was right outside my door.

The words "home" and "California" have always been synonymous for me. You see, I am a native Californian and for much of my life I have not considered this to be a remarkable piece of information—just a basic fact, like saying my eyes are blue and my hair is brown. But over the past decade, as I've traveled more extensively, I've come to realize this is one of the most important pieces of information about me. It informs everything I do. And through travel, I have realized other things as well. One is that saying I am Californian is shorthand to easily connect with anyone. Why? Because almost everyone has a very strong and positive idea about what "California" is. I'm not just talking about California the place; I'm talking about the dream. Utter the word "California" to people and their faces light up as they drift off to a dreamland that generally involves beaches and perpetual sunshine. And yet, as I watched this phenomenon take place time and again, I began to feel a bit exasperated. I wanted to stop their "California Dreaming" so I could share with them how this place is more than sun, surf, and happy people frolicking on the beach. Yes, all that is a part of it, but California is more than that. California is deeper.

I found myself digging into these thoughts even further when I visited Japan a few years ago. The Japanese have an intense interest in California that is very culturally specific. And while our loves overlapped quite a bit, I remember thinking of all the things and people I thought they had overlooked. There should be a book on California by a Californian, I thought. But what exactly would that look like, and what was it that I thought everyone was missing anyhow?

Growing up in the Santa Clara Valley (now more commonly known as Silicon Valley), I always felt very much outside of the "California Dream." Yes, I lived in California but I fit absolutely no stereotype of the California girl. In fact, I was quite an oddball. But I thrived in California because of that fact. I didn't realize it until much later, but California loves the stubborn individualist. Its history is built around them and its nurturing energy draws them in. From the Gold Rush to the movie industry, Silicon Valley to biotech, this state has been a siren call to dreamers with the will to work hard and the drive to stick with it longer than anyone normally would. I have quietly observed throughout my life how so many inventions, ideas, and social movements that began in California eventually reach out to a wider public and, much of the time, have changed the world. Just think of Levi Strauss making that first pair of blue jeans for those intrepid dreamers searching for gold during the Gold Rush in the mid-1800s. Or D. W. Griffith and Cecil B. DeMille, who decided to travel to a sunny village called Hollywood to experiment with the then-new invention of motion pictures in the early 1910s. Of course, their work wouldn't be possible without the first photographic motion studies, made by Eadweard Muybridge in 1886 a bit farther north in the town of Palo Alto, using Stanford University founder Leland Stanford's prizewinning racehorse. Less than two miles away and about fifty years later, William Hewlett and David Packard began toiling away in a garage making their first product, an audio oscillator. This humble spot is considered the birthplace of Silicon Valley and we all know how the innovations created there have profoundly changed our lives. Yet before it was Silicon Valley, it was called the Valley of Heart's Delight and was an oasis of fruit orchards and agriculture. The fertile land of California still produces two-thirds of the United States' agricultural food supply and has led the way in organic farming techniques since the 1970s. But already in 1947 there was a maverick farmer named Russell Wolters, who began farming organically in Carmel Valley. I could go on and on because the list is endless, yet for all these innovations, they all began with people just like you and me. California might be the place where change happens, but the agents of this change are its people. Theirs was the story I wanted to share.

Every book is a pilgrimage, and as I set out on this one, I was not completely sure where it would take me—that is one of the best parts of the adventure. I had a short list of people I knew were right for the book, with Alice Waters and Kay Sekimachi being at the very top. But as I dug into the research, I quickly began to lose my way in the sheer vastness of California itself. Tech, agriculture, aerospace, music, film, biotech—the list of industries that California is known for and in which it has led the way is very long and incredibly engrossing. However much I would have loved to include someone from each of these industries, my efforts to do so almost derailed this book completely. Simply put, I lost my focus. It took a box of old family photos to bring me back, and one picture in particular, of my mother, sister, and me in Yosemite in 1972, with Yosemite Falls in the background (page 6—that is me on the left, in pink). Until I was thirteen, the only vacation my family ever took was to Yosemite National Park. Every year in early May, before the tourists would descend on the park for summer, my parents would take my sister and me out of school and we would head there for our annual trip. These experiences were pivotal for me in every way. Seeing that old family photo re-sparked the overwhelming rush of inspiration I had had in Japan. It reminded me of what I wanted to share about California in the first place. It wasn't every industry of California—it was my California. The one that little two-year-old me was just beginning to know in that picture. The one I have experienced living my life here. And I would share that by sharing the people who have touched my own life in many different ways.

Most I have long admired from afar, like poet Robinson Jeffers, chef and activist Alice Waters, and artist/architect Roy McMakin. And some I have been lucky enough to meet along the path of my life, like artist Kay Sekimachi and Heath Ceramics owners Cathy Bailey and Robin Petravic. Yet each embodies the trait I identify most with as a Californian—a tenacious determination to pursue his or her passion creatively and without compromise. Through their pursuits, each has had an impact on the world, whether it is how we eat, how we create, how we perceive the world or how we interact within it. Their impact is undoubtedly global but when I am in their homes, the personal is brought back into focus. Extraordinary though these people are, they live their lives like most everyone else, their homes a series of rooms—living room, kitchen, bathroom, bedroom. And it is through these rooms and the details I find within them that their stories are told. Each home—each person—is rich in details.

As meaningful or beautiful as the details so often are, not all can be included in the book. As I photograph a house, I wear many hats—artist and photographer first, but also writer, historian, preservationist, pseudo biographer, ardent fan, and complete design geek too. Editing the hundreds of images down to the mere twenty or so that will share each person and his or her home story in a compelling and beautiful chapter is one of the challenges of making these books. So many of my favorite images—and the stories that go along with them—get left on the cutting room floor. But a few portrayed details of such poignancy, mystery, or history that I included them here.

Robinson Jeffers's home was full of incredible details and I shot them all. Tiny sculptures, minerals, and odd stones embedded into the walls of his home and garden walkways, sayings painted onto cabinets and above doors or carved into walls, hand-carved wood and stone animal totems throughout the house and tower—I knew from the start that I would be lucky to include a fraction of what was there in the chapter. "Hardy 1.11.28" is etched on a stone next to their kitchen door leading to the outside (page 9). The couple were so bereft when they learned their favorite writer and poet, Thomas Hardy, had died that they etched the date of his death in tribute. This act of reverence and its placement led me to think it was more than likely they touched that stone every time they walked out the door—a touchstone both figuratively and literally. One mirror in the living room was the subject of an inordinate number of images (I tend to overshoot objects I really love). It was fogged by age and, for some reason, as I looked into it, I felt its reflection held a deeper truth. It was like Jeffers and his wife, Una, were on the other side, watching me with approval. Even now as I look at one particular photograph of the mirror (page 9), I expect to see Jeffers sitting on the bench by the window looking back at me from its reflection.

Sometimes, I hold on to the mystery of not knowing about an object—as my experience photographing Alice Waters's bedroom can attest. Sitting on one of the windows was a tiny black-and-white slide of an old master painting, backlit by the sun (page 10). The painting was familiar, but I had to wait to look it up until days after my shoot to learn it was Velázquez's most famous painting, Las Meninas. Why was it there and what meaning did it hold? I have no idea. Every time I thought about emailing Waters to get the backstory, I always stopped myself. I love the wondering about it too much. A different kind of wonder is held in another image from Waters's bedroom. It is one of my favorite images from the entire making of this book, but most would consider it a mistake. Water's home was one where the quality of dappled, shadowy sunlight made photographing it a complete joy and arduous challenge all at once. Each room had its own special feel, with her bedroom enveloped in a green cast from the wisteria growing outside its windows—so beautiful yet uniquely difficult to shoot. The light

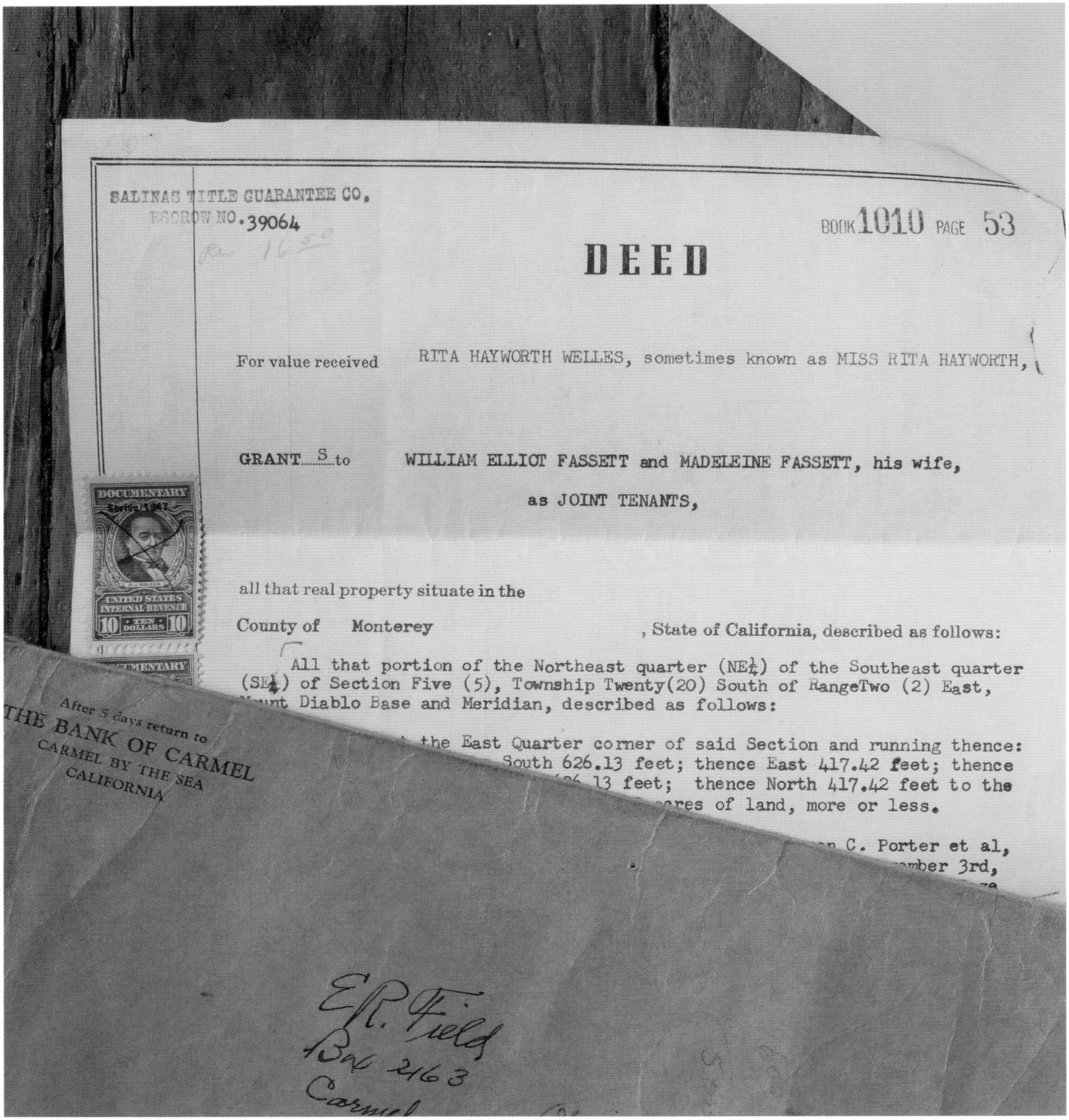

SALINAS TITLE GUARANTEE CO.
ESCROW NO. 39064

Rev 16⁵⁰

DEED

For value received   RITA HAYWORTH WELLES, sometimes known as MISS RITA HAYWORTH,

GRANT S to   WILLIAM ELLIOT FASSETT and MADELEINE FASSETT, his wife,

as JOINT TENANTS,

all that real property situate in the

County of   Monterey   , State of California, described as follows:

All that portion of the Northeast quarter (NE¼) of the Southeast quarter
(SE¼) of Section Five (5), Township Twenty(20) South of RangeTwo (2) East,
Mount Diablo Base and Meridian, described as follows:

the East Quarter corner of said Section and running thence:
South 626.13 feet; thence East 417.42 feet; thence
626.13 feet; thence North 417.42 feet to the
acres of land, more or less.

C. Porter et al,
mber 3rd,

DOCUMENTARY
UNITED STATES
INTERNAL REVENUE
10 TEN DOLLARS 10

After 5 days return to
THE BANK OF CARMEL
CARMEL BY THE SEA
CALIFORNIA

E.R. Field
Box 2163
Carmel

in that room was only optimal for a brief time so it was necessary to shoot rather quickly. As I did, I inadvertently double-exposed one of the images on the roll of film (page 13). When I got my film back, I was more excited about this image than almost any other and it remains an absolute favorite. It miraculously holds within its frame all the delicate beauty of the light and room, as well as my frenzied experience shooting it. Of course, it makes no sense in Alice's chapter but still, what a beautiful image.

On occasion images that hold important historical resonance don't even make the final edit. In the case of this book, a deed and a light plate would have been casualties were they not included here. My photograph of the original Nepenthe property deed signed by Rita Hayworth or, as it reads, "Rita Hayworth Welles, sometimes known as Miss Rita Hayworth," felt like an incredibly important historical artifact of the family's story and a bit of Hollywood history to boot. The Fassett family were kind enough to pull it out of safekeeping for me so I could shoot it but alas, I couldn't find a way to work the deed into their chapter (page 14). A different type of history is told in a photograph from Charles Moore's home of a scratched gray light plate revealing vibrant royal-blue paint underneath (page 16). Moore's condo led to a more complex chapter because it is now a rental, so I had many questions as to what was original to when Moore was in residence and what had changed since his death (amazingly, it is almost all original to Moore himself). As I researched and interviewed those who knew him, over and again I kept hearing the comment that the bright blue of the window-seat cushions could not be original to Moore, as it competes with the view of the landscape—a fundamental shift from the ethos of the Sea Ranch. Through researching vintage photographs of the space, I found that the cushions had in fact been at first a more subtle gray-blue. But Moore was known to change things in his condo quite a lot, and as I suspected, the vintage images reflected many different incarnations of the space, with different wall colors and décor. That blue light plate I am sure was one of Moore's changes, and is evidence of where the idea for royal blue cushions had come from. But even though no one can definitively say when those cushions had been changed to that brighter blue (before Moore's death or after), I have to admit, I really love them ("original" or not). And I especially love the thought that Moore possibly defied the famous Sea Ranch ethos when it suited his needs. He kept his home true to his own needs first— an unabashed original.

This idea of originality, grounded in a deep respect of self, is a hallmark of California, as I hope this book will attest. As you move through each chapter and enter the personal universe of each inspiring

INTERIOR PORTRAITS

Californian, of course glean as much design and interiors inspiration as you can—it goes without saying that these homes are unique and special from a design point of view. But also look deeper. The homes of these Californians are not just interiors but portraits of their inner, creative worlds where their dreams have been nurtured and have grown. Wikipedia links the term "California Dream" to the Gold Rush of 1849 and "the psychological motivation to gain fast wealth and fame in a new land." This may well have been true many years ago. But as you can see from the lives lived within the beautiful walls throughout these pages, the dream of California is rooted in far deeper ground than that antiquated definition. When I began the journey of this book, a small part of me worried that I was searching for a California that may no longer exist. But each person featured in these pages—with his or her home, life, and work—has reaffirmed that the California I love, the one that I have known all my life, is still here. It's a California Dream composed of bred-in-the-bone individualism, creativity, and originality, made real through love, hard work, and dedication. And it is still thriving.

ALMA
ALLEN

—

JOSHUA TREE

When I first learned that artist Alma Allen (b. 1970) lived out in the desert near Joshua Tree National Park, it made me feel that there was order and sense in the universe. I breathed a sigh and thought, "Of course, he does…" His work always felt to me as if it somehow occurred in another atmosphere, so if it was not created on the moon, then the California desert was the next best alternative. I had found my way to Alma through the furniture he designed and made earlier in his career. I am a sucker for beautifully carved wood pieces, and Alma's always felt to me above and beyond anything I was seeing elsewhere. The shapes were elemental, the craftsmanship impeccable, and, most importantly, when I looked at the pieces I felt transported—no doubt to my imaginary lunar world of Alma. Born in Utah, he had a very unconventional and arduous path toward becoming a celebrated artist embraced by the art world. Highlights (if you can call them that) of his early life include running away from his home at sixteen, doing construction work and barely scraping by, and moving to New York City only to break his leg and, unable to pay his rent, nearly lose his apartment. Of course, these things did not happen one right after the other (thankfully), but as I looked at his trajectory, those tough moments appear to have yielded the turning points in his life. In needing to pay his rent, he took the little sculptures of wood and stone that he had compulsively been carving since childhood and sold them from an ironing board on the street in SoHo. His buyers turned out to be some of the most notable artists, designers, and collectors of the time. And from that, Alma's work began to be collected—and, most essentially, to support him financially. When he developed a debilitating case of carpal tunnel syndrome that could not be remedied despite multiple surgeries, he bought a huge (and very expensive) robot originally used in auto manufacturing and refashioned it to carve for him. From this, his work leaped from small-scale to larger-scale pieces, like the three included in the 2014 Whitney Biennial. This show, considered his big break, undeniably opened up opportunities for him. Yet as I drove up the dirt road to his home where he has lived for over a decade, I felt a deep relief that he had settled in the remoteness of the desert. I had only met him briefly before this first visit, but my overwhelming sense was that despite all the hardships, which suggest a true toughness of character, there is an equally delicate side to him that needs a very particular environment to thrive. Clearly the desert is it.

The home and studio that he designed and built curl around an enclosed central courtyard, so the grouping of buildings feels a bit like a compound. Each structure is made of cinderblock, concrete, and wood with two large walls of sliding glass as the front entrance. This front "door" is actually on the backside of the property, butting right up to the desert wilderness. The living space is simple and essential—a combined kitchen and living room, a small utility area, and a bedroom with a master bath all opening out to the central courtyard. As I began to shoot, Alma looked at the living room area and said a little forlornly, "This will all be gone soon." The room was filled with Alma's work—large and small—and peppered with flea market finds and an African bench. But most of his work here was destined for the two solo gallery shows he was working on at the time or had already been sold to collectors. Although he has kept a few small pieces over the years because they are personal favorites, the large pieces are generally sold and leave to live elsewhere. The dining table is an exception to this, mainly because it was used in his studio for years and is patched up. Alma laughed about the pink seams of putty that are clearly visible, but I rather liked the table more for its scars. Mismatched chairs, including a rattan beauty recently found at a thrift store, surround the long table, and down its center are more bits and bobs—candleholders, bowls, little sculptures, and more—that all seem to be of Alma's doing. After a while, I found myself trying to figure out what he did not make, since virtually every collection on his shelves and tabletops was definitely from planet Alma. A bench in the small utility area leading to the bedroom had twin street-find sculptures basking in the sun and in the bedroom I spotted an Eileen Gray E1027 table, a George Nelson cabinet, and a pair of watercolors by his girlfriend, the artist and writer Su Wu. But besides these, it was hard to find anything not by his hand. I especially liked his ingenious rope towel holder that hangs down from the bathroom ceiling. It struck me as brilliant, utilitarian, and possibly the best reuse for dormant rock-climbing gear ever.

Down the pathway across the central courtyard sits the combined office and studio. If I was overwhelmed by the collections in the house, the sheer volume of small pieces found on the bookshelves in this space is a complete jaw dropper. As I looked closely through the shelves, among work that I recognized easily as Alma's were more rudimentary carvings. There were even a couple of handmade arrows—one with a face—that Alma had made when he was a boy. Mixed in with more current work were pieces he had carved as a teenager out of furniture scraps. The evolution of shapes I so closely identify with Alma's particularly beautiful universe started very young. Its trajectory lies here on these shelves.

INTERIOR PORTRAITS

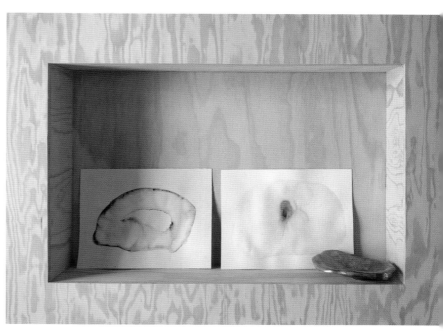

INTERIOR PORTRAITS

ROBINSON JEFFERS

———

CARMEL

've long considered Robinson Jeffers (1887-1962) a quintessential Californian so the fact that he is not more widely known and admired escapes me. Arguably one of the most significant poets of the twentieth century and an icon of the environmental movement, I first came across him in a poetry-frenzied phase when I was sixteen years old. Sitting on the floor of my favorite bookstore/coffeehouse I was drawn in by his moody portrait on the cover of one of his books. His poetry was epic, sometimes dark, and rooted in a deep connection to the natural world and more specifically the California landscape. Although my poetry phase was short-lived, Jeffers's biographical notes stuck with me. They painted a picture of the life he lived with his family in a stone house in Carmel, California, from 1919 until his death in 1962. Carmel was only an hour away from where I was growing up, and I marveled at the list of visitors his family had to their home at a time when getting there would have been a challenge at best—Edna St. Vincent Millay, Charlie Chaplin, Charles Lindbergh, George Gershwin, and Martha Graham to name just a few. My young mind was set alight wondering about their life on the seashore. It took nearly twenty-five years before I found myself visiting Jeffers's home and it reignited that curiosity I had felt before. From it, a love and respect for both Jeffers and his wife, Una, have only grown. I've come to see them as the personification of many of the qualities of life in California that I find myself most connected to—specifically, living and creating in the very truth of one's beliefs.

It is clear when delving into the facts of Jeffers's life that there were two defining moments that irrevocably shaped his life and work. The first was meeting a woman named Una Call Kuster at the University of Southern California in 1906. He would later marry her after a bit of a scandal (she was already married when they met). The second was the couple's decision to move to Carmel. Jeffers has said that when they arrived, they had found their "inevitable place." In early 1919, now with twin boys, they bought some land on a rocky promontory and set about building the home where they would live and create for the rest of their lives. A stone house inspired by an English cottage, it was built from granite rocks hauled up from the beach. Although they had contracted a builder to do the work, after a time Jeffers signed on as his apprentice to learn how to lay stone himself. After the house was complete and at Una's request, he went on to build a stone tower in the garden. He named it Hawk Tower after a hawk that circled overhead every day of the four years it took him to build it. When it was finished, Jeffers carved their spirit animals over their own doors to the tower, a unicorn over hers and a hawk over his.

Today, with the encroaching Carmel neighborhood tight to the property line, it is hard to imagine that when the Jefferses moved here they were moving out of town, to live in a place where the sounds of the sea and the wind were their only neighbors. The street that now follows the coastline was then a mere pathway, and beyond it, where their home would eventually sit, no trees grew, just a grassy hillside. In fact, Jeffers planted all the cypress and eucalyptus trees that still grow throughout the neighborhood. Entering the living room, I was overwhelmed by the most wonderful sense that this was a happy family home. Paneled in redwood with seating centered around the hearth, the room held not one but two pianos, with window seats at the far end of the room for reading or just staring out the window to the sea. It was easy to imagine the family here on quiet evenings, either reading or playing music together—a view of domestic life that has long past. Of course, Una did have some other ways to while away her time, as the skull in a cabinet above the hearth will attest. She was known to have a séance every now and again. The small bedroom off the living room has hand-painted writing above the closet door: "Bien Faire et Laissez Dire." This is the first evidence of the little sayings that are painted throughout the house—a conversation between Jeffers, Una, and their family. Originally used as a guest room (the family slept in a small attic room), this bedroom was always intended—and ultimately used by Jeffers—as the place where they would leave this world when their times came. He even wrote "The Bed by the Window" about it with the darkly amusing line about how their houseguest "…hardly suspects."

The kitchen opens up to an exposed-beam ceiling and is filled with Jeffers's and Una's animal totems tucked into cabinets, hanging from banners, and even carved on the china hutch. Hanging high on one wall appears to be a long animal tusk. Una's obsession with unicorns was so intense that she ordered a narwhal tusk (the unicorn of the sea) from a mail-order catalog, intending to use it as a walking stick. But when it arrived it was so heavy that the only thing to do was to hang it on the wall. Across a small garden sits the stone tower Jeffers built for Una. Each of them had a room—Jeffers on the ground floor, Una's above it, and the roof looked out to the Pacific. They were a perfect match—he a writer who loved his solitude and she the more social of the two with a gift for wrangling the attention his work brought to their door. And come to their door it did. Finally, they hung out a sign on the gate that bent the truth just a touch—"Not at home before 4 p.m." The kindest way possible to keep room for what was most important—family and Jeffers's writing.

KAY
SEKIMACHI

—

BERKELEY

To hear the story of the first time textile artist Kay Sekimachi (b. 1926) laid her eyes on a loom, it sounds a lot like love at first sight. The year was 1949 and Kay was taking a few art classes at the California College of Arts and Crafts in Oakland. As she walked by a textile class in session, the moving and swaying of the students working on their looms stopped her in her tracks. After that, she scrounged up her last $150 and bought a loom for herself. And the rest, as they say, is history. Frequently called the "weaver's weaver," Kay is widely considered a pioneer of the post-World War II fiber art movement and is credited with helping to resurrect weaving as a legitimate form of artistic expression. Throughout her career, her work has pushed the boundaries of her medium, much of it now sitting in the collections of institutions like the Smithsonian and San Francisco's de Young Museum and exhibited throughout the world.

A second-generation Japanese American born in San Francisco, her childhood was not without hardships, most notably the death of her father in 1937 and being interned with her family during World War II. Yet art making was a constant throughout her young life and, after her discovery of the loom, she was determined to make weaving her profession. A key turning point came when she attended a lecture by weaver Trude Guermonprez, who had studied under Bauhaus-trained Benita Koch-Otte. Guermonprez would become her most important teacher. As Sekimachi puts it, she "opened my eyes to what weaving could be." In particular, she deepened Kay's understanding of the double weave, which became the basis for her career-defining three-dimensional monofilament pieces of the early 1960s. These fluid sculptures were how I first discovered Sekimachi's work. A friend had one hanging in his studio and I was fascinated with it as it swayed in the breeze from an open window. It moved like an underwater creature. At the time, I was working on a project about the mid-twentieth-century crafts movement, so my friend was kind enough to make an introduction.

Walking through Kay's front door that first time, I was completely taken by surprise. A discreet 1895 Victorian duplex on the outside, the inside is anything but. Kay and her late husband, legendary woodturner Bob Stocksdale (1913-2003), had the interiors remodeled in 1979 by a family friend, the architect Albert Lanier, who was the husband of artist Ruth Asawa. He transformed their home into a light-filled open-plan space with an upstairs aerie and small bedroom tucked in the back. The home has served as Sekimachi's creative cocoon for the past forty-plus years and is filled with a lifetime of work—both hers and Bob's—mixed with that of friends and peers alike. Pieces by legendary woodworkers George Nakashima and Sam Maloof commingle with a simple couch in the main living area. Surrounding these are various

Japanese tansu cabinets whose every surface is arranged with an assemblage of artwork, nature's ephemera, or mix of the two. The dining area features a Sam Maloof dining table and chairs as its centerpiece, a wedding present from the woodworker to his best friend, Bob. The bookcase along the wall holds examples of Stocksdale's finished bowls in every size, while above the stove in the small kitchen sits a grouping of bowls that were left unfinished when he passed in 2003. Kay's work has always been rooted in and inspired by the natural world so it was not completely surprising to see a big hornet's nest hanging from the ceiling. Kay's voice was filled with both astonishment and delight as she shared that a friend sent it to her in the mail from Vermont by surprise a decade ago. The intention had been for Kay to use it for the hornet's-nest bowls she was making at the time but she deemed it too beautiful and perfect to dismantle. It has hung in her kitchen ever since.

Up on the second floor is a mezzanine work area with a nice daybed for the occasional nap. Originally Kay's main work studio, now the space stores much of Kay and Bob's archives. During my visit, her early student work and weavings were sitting out, ready to go to the de Young Museum for a show of her life's work. Dangling from the highest point of the ceiling were a couple of her exquisite monofilament pieces that she was repairing for their respective owners and a series of her "twine line" sculptures pinned behind them to the wall. More tansu chests here held even more of her collections from years of beachcombing in Hawaii. She began incorporating these treasures into jewelry about ten years ago and now has a dedicated workstation directly below, across from the kitchen. But where are the looms, I wondered? "Oh, they are in the weaving annex," she said as she led me out the back door and across the deck. A small, separate room holds two looms, both dressed and mid-project. A Danish chest sits at the back of the room, filled with more collections from the sea. Sea urchins of every shape fill one drawer and another holds a massive piece of coral and the vertebrae of some small mammal. Every drawer is meticulously ordered by type and color. Propped up on the wall were tall wood contraptions with pegs and knobs that look fascinating, but what they are used for I had no idea. Kay informed me they were frames for various weaving techniques but pointed out the tallest contraption as a special one. Bob made it to her specification in his basement woodshop so she could work at a larger scale. Looking at the two looms, I asked if either one was that original purchase she had made in 1949. She answered, "No, these are eight-harness looms. That first one was a four-harness. But I still have it downstairs in my weaving storage. I tell you, that was the best one hundred and fifty dollars I ever spent."

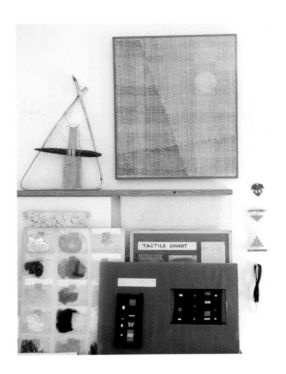

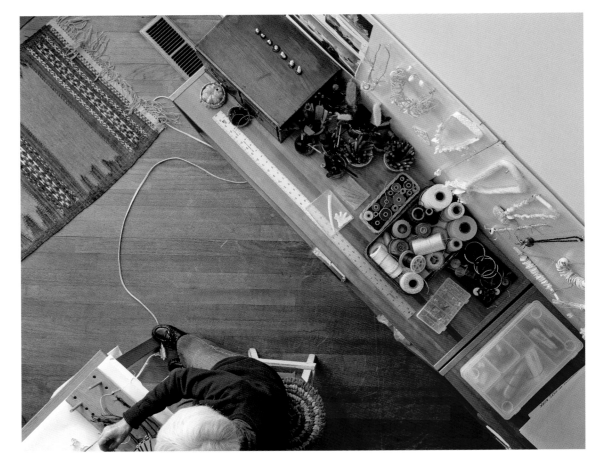

ROY
MCMAKIN

—

SAN DIEGO

'‍ve always found Roy McMakin (b. 1956) to be an enigmatic figure in the worlds of art, design, and architecture. I could never figure out how he has successfully straddled all three for more than four decades in a time when we regularly pigeonhole people into just one. "It's because I tend to say yes," he told me. Yes to starting a furniture design company in Los Angeles with a friend in the late 1980s. Yes to designing his first architecture project. All these yeses as he maintained an art practice that began in his college years at the University of California at San Diego. Always a creative child, he grew up in the Midwest and in Denver, and his interest in the meaning of objects began at an early age. Yet his time in San Diego was pivotal. It informed his conceptual art making and helped him realize that his interest in furniture was not so much in the making of it but in the ideas imbued within it. And it was in San Diego where he first encountered the architecture of neo-modernist Irving J. Gill—a constant and profound influence on his own work ever since. He jokes that he had to leave California (for Seattle, where he lived for seventeen years) because his obsession with Gill was so intense that he "couldn't break up with him and stay in the same town." Yet Southern California always felt like home, so in 2011, he moved back. Unsurprisingly, the thing that sealed the deal for the return was the rental of an Irving Gill house he had always loved. By the time I visited him to photograph his home, he had moved out of that house and was deep into building the home he intends to live in for the rest of his life.

It took some convincing for Roy to allow me to photograph the little one-bedroom rental that he and his husband, Mike, are living in while he designs and builds their "forever house" a few blocks away. I totally understood why. Roy's aesthetic is so finely honed and intertwined with "home" that an interim rental must have felt like a big departure from what he would generally share. He warned me that it was tiny, and therefore not as "minimal" as he usually lives; however, having seen only one beautiful scouting picture before I arrived at his door, as soon as I walked in, I knew I had been right to persist. Overlooking a canyon in central San Diego, the home felt like a distillation of his life in objects and colors—and all held within the walls of a home he might have lived in while in college. It is as if he were visiting and reconnecting with his past while creating his "forever" future. Entering the living room, I recognized Roy's iconic Slat-Back chairs surrounding the dining table, with a Gustav Stickley chest of drawers behind it. The room is wood paneled with a brick fireplace, and windows wrap around three walls, making it feel a bit like a tree house. The built-in bookshelves in one corner are filled with every possible style of vintage Bauer pottery, grouped by color—the most populous being the green-hued pieces, to the point where they overflow to another hutch next to the kitchen. Roy mentioned that the Bauer vases are part of his "re-California-ing" that he has been in the midst of since returning. He had purged himself of all his Bauer when he left for Washington, and now that he's back, he has found himself longing for it again.

Roy left me in the house to shoot for the day, telling me to make myself at home, so I moved slowly with the light, often getting absorbed in looking at the details of his paintings and objects. A still-life painting by the artist (and Roy's former professor) Manny Farber sits propped above the fireplace; a ceramic bowl, vase, and crock that sit atop the chest of drawers are combined in different line drawings tacked to the wall for an upcoming gallery show. The most poignant corner of the house is behind the dining table, where two beat-up toy horses sit on the floor as if they are gazing out the window. I asked about them and Roy shared a story about their dog named Joan, who had passed away. In the latter part of her life she had gone blind, and Roy affectionately described her as having a rather "cantankerous" personality. She could not see a thing, yet every day she would scamper to that corner and deliberately knock down those horses and it would give her a cranky satisfaction. So Roy leaves them there as a tribute and reminder.

The tiny bedroom is down a short hallway off the kitchen. The room has just enough space for a bed and three vintage dressers in the same shade of green along one wall. Mike's antique rolltop desk fits as if it was made for the small nook next to the door; atop the desk sits a light with a hunting dog on its base, and landscape paintings cover the walls. Many of the objects and paintings in this corner he casually mentioned were from his early thrift-shopping days when he was a teenager in Denver. I couldn't help but wish I had had such a great eye at fourteen. Easily my favorite "room" in the house is the sun porch, which runs the length of the living room. It is half covered, half exposed to the sun, and Roy has set it up as a sort of combined solarium, sleeping porch, and guest bedroom. He generally works at the table here every morning until the sun gets too hot. By the looks of it, it is the favorite room of their dogs, Margaret and Kevin, too. They were napped out on the bed here for most of my time photographing the house. By day's end, I felt a bit jealous of them. Surrounded by plants and with plenty of pillows on the daybed to snuggle into, this sun porch really is the most perfect spot.

INTERIOR PORTRAITS

INTERIOR PORTRAITS

INTERIOR PORTRAITS

RAY KAPPE

PACIFIC PALISADES

Since the early twentieth century, the Los Angeles area has been a hotbed of influential and innovative architecture. Frank Lloyd Wright, Richard Neutra, Rudolph Schindler, Greene and Greene, Thom Mayne, Frank Gehry, not to mention the architects of the Case Study House program—the list of architects that made a mark here is daunting. Ray Kappe (b. 1927) sits easily among these luminaries, yet his place in this group is singular and distinctive. Best known for his expansive glass-and-wood homes whose integration with the landscape epitomizes California living, his impact as a pioneer of green architecture and as an educator and innovator in the world of architecture education has also been remarkable. In fact, after being the founding director of the architecture department at California State Polytechnic University at Pomona in 1968, Ray decided to break away in the belief that there was a better way to teach and learn. With a group of colleagues and students, he founded a new school in 1972, SCI-Arc, or the Southern California Institute of Architecture, that was dedicated to a more experimental and hands-on learning environment, as it continues to be to this day.

The first time I showed up on his doorstep was in 2009. I was in the midst of my first book and was thrilled to photograph his home for it. My experience there that first shoot was pivotal for me, and it is etched in my memory not only for the joy I felt shooting their home (it is so much better in person!!) but also because of the chats I had with Ray's wife, Shelly, an architecture educator and writer in her own right. Talk about a formidable design couple! Their combination—Ray with his deep, sonorous voice matched with Shelly and her dancing, kind eyes and effervescent and curious personality—had me completely charmed and inspired by the two of them and the life they had created. The fact that their chapter ended up being cut from the book at the last minute has always saddened me (the cruelty of a limited page count). Of course now I realize it was some sort of divine intervention because this book would not be complete without them.

Returning to photograph a home numerous times over the years is a special gift. Houses, like people, are living a life and I was excited to reacquaint myself with not only both Ray and Shelly, but also their home. Memories of my first visit flooded back the second I heard the sound of trickling water as I walked up their front steps. I had forgotten that their home was built over an underground spring that surfaces halfway up their property near the front door. It was one of the challenges of the site that inspired Ray's brilliant design of anchoring the structure on six concrete towers, so the house looks as if it is tiptoeing up the hill. Arriving at the front door brings you directly under the main floor of the house. The sensation of it hovering overhead makes walking into the Kappes' home feel a lot like entering a space ship, and the impact (I imagine) is just as stunning. Ascending up the central staircase past Ray's ground-floor studio and into the main living area, the house blooms out into an expansive, multilevel living space. This home is the definition of most people's fantasies of California living. Mine included. Its main living areas—upper living room, lower living room, dining room, and kitchen—are all open to each other yet afford little corners that feel cozy and private. The way light plays and the integration of the home with nature is equally alluring. The two wings of sleeping quarters, the kids' rooms at the back of the house and the master bedroom toward the front feel like very private satellites that can either exist independently or integrate into the whole of the house when desired: a detail that seemed doubly important as Ray is more of an early bird and Shelly, a night owl. They had not changed a bit in the years that had passed since my first visit, and Ray and I chatted as I took some portraits of him in the kitchen having his morning tea. He shared stories about Richard Neutra's temperament (fascinating to hear) and his one experience working with photographer Julius Shulman which re-illustrated just how integral a part Ray has been to the architectural fabric of Los Angeles for over sixty years. He is certainly an éminence grise now. Just a few days before I was there, Ray and Shelly had welcomed a group of Australian architecture students to tour the house. Tours are a common occurrence for them, living in an award-winning architectural masterpiece as they do.

The entire time I was there this second visit, I looked for subtle changes to the house but could only find a few. The royal-blue upholstery seemed a bit more vibrant—no doubt they had gotten new cushion covers made—and Ray's studio had a laptop computer that I didn't think was there before. But otherwise it felt virtually the same. As I was finishing up, Shelly emerged from the master bedroom and we talked about the European houses I had shot for my second book. She and Ray had been to practically every single house on their family vacations and had created complete slide shows of each so they could teach the houses to their students at SCI-Arc. We are talking the 1970s and 1980s, when Ray, Shelly, and their three kids would go and knock on a door and ask for a tour from the owners. She pointed to carousels of slides and asked me what I thought the best way would be to archive them. I swear, I wanted to have a slide show right then and there. I said something about their needing to be scanned, but as I drove away that day (and many times since), I fantasized about archiving these slides with them myself. Can you imagine the stories?

INTERIOR PORTRAITS

INTERIOR PORTRAITS

MADELEINE FITZPATRICK & EVAN SHIVELY

SHIVELY

—

MARSHALL

The first time I made my way to Evan Shively (b. 1964) and Madeleine Fitzpatrick's (b. 1958) place through the ranchlands of Petaluma, I had no idea what I was in for. I had known about each separately through various mutual friends for some time—Evan for being an incredible chef, artist, and dealer of massive pieces of wood at his large wood emporium, Arborica, and Madeleine for her gifts as a painter and healer (most notably for the artist Sam Francis). I had been told their place was "amazing," but let's face it, that word is overused and open to vastly different interpretations. I was up for the adventure, though, and the drive was sublime that warm day with rolling green hills and birds chirping away in the sun. So I followed their directions (GPS doesn't work here), turned onto the dirt road, and found myself in front of a huge eucalyptus trunk with an entry cut into it like a gateway to an enchanted garden. My first visit was not a long one, but it was deeply memorable. "Amazing" wasn't an understatement, but I left worried. These two live in a place of wonder and embody everything I love about creative people in California. Their world is very much "more is more"—the land, their home, the food, even the smell of the flowers in their garden. It was as if they knew the secret of how to step inside things and turn them up to their ultimate deliciousness. Everything was just so sublime it seemed impossible to think a photographic image could really capture it all. It took me months to process that first visit and mull how I would contain all of it in a chapter. But of course I would return. I had to.

As I approached the eucalyptus gateway on my second visit, three massive dogs came bounding over to greet me. Evan and Madeleine's home is essentially two metal warehouses. In the 1980s, they were the dormitories for the Synanon cult (or drug rehabilitation center, depending on who is telling the story). Evan and Madeline found this spot for their art studios in 1992. Five years later they decided to live here full time and have slowly been transforming the spaces ever since. They bridged the original warehouses with a translucent structure that is easily the most unexpected entrance hall I've ever experienced. Wood double doors open into a greenhouse teeming predominantly with bromeliads and orchids—two of Evan's obsessions—but also ferns and even a trickling water feature that is home to a disturbingly large salamander. To the back of this solarium is their kitchen, filled with restaurant-grade equipment of every type. For years, Evan and Madeleine had a catering business famous for a traveling wood-fired pizza oven that would go wherever the party was going to be (it now sits happily in their yard). Food is central to their life here, and the heart of the home is this kitchen greenhouse. I was lucky enough to enjoy a few of the best meals of my life while I was here. On a break from shooting, I sat at the kitchen counter as Evan seasoned some chicken for the outdoor grill and I remember marveling at just how many different dashes of this and splashes of that he used. It was simultaneously an improvisation and a very precise chemistry that he was creating, the kind that can only come from a knowledge of food and flavor that has been studied and lived from the inside out. The house is a similarly eccentric composition. Both warehouses have been transformed into spaces that are somehow more like stage sets in which they live than a domestic interior. My eyes widened when I entered the room that houses their dining and living room. It is literally draped entirely in silver Mylar, save for the floor. I asked Madeleine what gave her the idea to do this and she completely surprised me with the most practical answer—Mylar is an insulating material and those warehouses get mighty cold. A small wood sculpture by British artist David Nash, a client and friend, sits on the dining table, and Madeleine's striking paintings hang on the walls. To call it a dramatic space feels like an understatement at best. The warehouse on the opposite side is equally theatrical: draped in a gauzy white material, it has a decidedly more loungy vibe. Low white couches draped with sheepskins are arranged in three seating areas, and there is even a bar off to the side. When I was there, pink naked ladies—a local wildflower—were at the height of their bloom and the room was filled with them and their fragrant scent. But for all the grandness Evan and Madeleine have created inside their home, the entire time I was there it was clear that their life revolved around being out of doors on the land with their animals and at Evan's Arborica, only a short walk away. Even on a Sunday, Evan was milling a massive walnut tree (by himself, I might add) that had just arrived from a neighborhood in Sacramento. When Madeleine is not in her painting studio, she is tending her tremendous garden filled with a wide variety of edible and medicinal herbs among the many other delicious things (she is known for her incredible salads containing up to one hundred different plants picked fresh from this yard). She told me to help myself to anything in the garden and I daresay I did. The raspberries were in abundance, so I gorged myself on them until my fingers (and parts of my camera) were stained red. One of their dogs stood watching my gluttonous display and, as our eyes locked, I snickered at the thought that he had no doubt witnessed this kind of thing before. It's easy to lose yourself to your senses here. It feels like the right thing to do.

INTERIOR PORTRAITS

INTERIOR PORTRAITS

Natural Fashion Tribal Decoration from Africa

THE FASSETT FAMILY

—

BIG SUR

Big Sur is a mythic site in California. A wild ninety-mile stretch of coastline from Carmel south to San Simeon, it is remote, shockingly beautiful, and has long attracted free spirits and creative souls alike. John Steinbeck, Robinson Jeffers, Henry Miller, Edward Weston, Jack Kerouac—they all were drawn here for its beauty and isolation and the freedom it afforded to live a creative life. William (1911-1992) and Madeleine Fassett (1911-1986)—or Bill and Lolly as they are known—were drawn here for much the same reason in 1947, and their creative expression was Nepenthe.

In the beginning, Nepenthe was a family enterprise centered around a log cabin and hospitality. Today the restaurant is still run by the Fassett family and has grown to include a café, gift shop, and a close community that keeps it going. I had known of Nepenthe for years—from watching Elizabeth Taylor and Richard Burton in *The Sandpiper* and from my own visits to enjoy its amazing views and rustic modern architecture. On my travels a few years ago, I visited an art exhibition of the painter Erin Lee Gafill in Gualala, California. She has a true gift for painting the California coast (especially its elusive fog), which only a fifth-generation Californian could have. As we talked, she mentioned that her family ran a restaurant in Big Sur and she lived in the cabin there. Could she mean Nepenthe, I thought…I had never noticed a cabin. But yes, that is exactly what she meant. Erin's family stories have afforded me a view into this place that has inspired me not only because it was the crossroads for all the creative titans who were drawn to the area, but also because it is a deeply Californian story, of hard work, determination, and a somewhat crazy dream.

The stories of Nepenthe are rich right from its beginning. The cabin that would become the Fassett family home had previously been bought on a whim by Hollywood legend Orson Welles and his then-new wife, starlet Rita Hayworth. But, as the Welles-Hayworth union was rather short-lived, the lovebirds never moved in and the cabin sat empty until the Fassetts inquired about it in the fall of 1947. The family bought it and quickly went about making it home. Big Sur at the time was not a very busy place. Highway 1 had opened just ten years before and was not heavily trafficked except in the summer. The full-time population was barely three hundred, and there was no electricity to speak of beyond the occasional generator (electricity came to the area in the mid-1950s). But within the first three days of the family's arrival, so many friends had stopped by their cabin that Bill suggested they start a restaurant. That is how Nepenthe began—simply a family needing a way to support itself. Yet Lolly's vision was grander than a mere restaurant. She envisioned an open-air pavilion for good food, dancing, community, and a place to forget the woes of daily life (*nepenthe* is believed to mean "isle of no care" in Greek). Her grand vision realized, Nepenthe remains at the heart of the Big Sur community for locals and visitors alike. Lolly's belief that the land and its spectacular views were a place meant to be shared has been its driving force, and the Fassett family still runs Nepenthe with this core ethos today.

When visiting the restaurant for the first time, it is easy to not even notice the original cabin above the terrace where Erin and her family now live. Bill and Lolly worked with architect Rowan Maiden, a student of Frank Lloyd Wright, to design the restaurant, and it is an impressive, high-ceilinged space that is oriented toward views of the surrounding land and coastline. It remains close to its original design today. The only major change was the addition of windows after the first winter—the open-air idea was not so workable with wind and rain. Directly next to the front entrance is the corner bar affectionately named "Dirty Corner" after the dirty limerick contests that would take place here between Bill and regulars like Henry Miller in the early days. The entrance to the cabin is hidden around back with a cheery blue gate to afford the family some privacy from wayward restaurant patrons. Clad in bricks on the outside, the inside is still a rustic log cabin. The grapevine Lolly planted continues to twist its way over the entrance, and the cabin is filled with generations of family photos and the paintings by Erin's grandmother's grandmother, Jane Gallatin Powers, wife of the founder of Carmel, Frank Powers. The cabin is small and it takes a stretch of the imagination to believe that a family of seven could have been raised here, let alone many of their offspring, but as Erin shares, the door was never closed to visitors in Lolly's day. In fact, the living room that now has a comfy couch and chair used to hold end-to-end beds that ran the length of the room and would function as a long couch to accommodate visitors throughout the day and even into the night. (For a while, the Fassetts had one of the only televisions in the area, so people would come by just to watch TV.)

Since Lolly's passing and the incredible growth in the popularity of Big Sur and Nepenthe in particular as a destination, life here has evolved. But its heart remains pure, and the history and those early days of artists and free spirits can still be found if you are just willing to dream a bit. The tourist traffic is formidable nowadays in the summer months, but go to Big Sur in the winter, when it is a bit dark and rainy and go to Nepenthe for dinner. On a stormy night, the restaurant is lit with candlelight and, as the surf pounds below, you can feel not only the spirit that is true Big Sur but also that of Bill and Lolly, who worked hard to share their beautiful land with everyone and keep this bit of rugged California alive and nurtured. It is a legacy that endures.

INTERIOR PORTRAITS

INTERIOR PORTRAITS

DONLYN LYNDON

SEA RANCH

cannot walk a trail at the Sea Ranch without hearing the voice of Donlyn Lyndon (b. 1936) in my head. It wasn't always this way, of course. I had visited and fallen in love with the Sea Ranch years before I sought him out for this book. But knowing him has been not only an immersive education in the roots of this architectural gem, but also like the best secret pass I never knew I should dream of. There is literally no better way to learn about a place than by getting an in-depth tour by one of its founders and creators—and that is who Donlyn is. The "L" in MLTW, the architectural firm responsible for one of the most important buildings at the Sea Ranch, he has remained involved in the life here and continues to help steward this special place, with its original intentions intact, into the future.

For those not familiar with it, the Sea Ranch is a ten-mile stretch of former ranchland on the Sonoma County coast in Northern California. In the early 1960s, it was planned as a new kind of housing development—one with its guiding light being to "live light on the land," a tenet adopted from the Pomo, a local Native American tribe. The landscape and sighting of the buildings was master planned by legendary modernist landscape architect Lawrence Halprin, and brought in to create the original buildings were MLTW, for the multi-unit structure (known as Condominium 1), and Joseph Esherick, for a grouping of single-family dwellings (known as the Hedgerow Houses). The Sea Ranch was completely groundbreaking in 1965 when it was unveiled to the world. Yet like so many places that have endured for fifty-plus years, it has changed a bit with time and I was eager to find those original places that still embodied its true essence. I had done my fair share of snooping around during my earlier visits, but hanging out with Donlyn for a day changed everything. His tour hit all the essential and original bits of the Sea Ranch—Condominium 1 (he got me into three of the ten units) as well as Moonraker and Ohlson Recreation Centers, which were pivotal from both architectural and landscape perspectives. We took an extensive walk on the trails, where he explained how homes were sited to never interfere with another's view and how the land had been broken up into large "rooms" with a central common landscape that would be free of building in perpetuity, thereby preserving the character of the original terrain. Donlyn even kept watch as I snuck into the men's locker room at Moonraker to see the last remaining fully original example of Barbara Stauffacher Solomon's Supergraphics—her well-known work another element that defines the Sea Ranch. It was the best tour I could have hoped for and I've included a few images from it to finish this chapter.

Donlyn's dedication and work with the Sea Ranch has been a constant in his life, yet his career has taken him far afield. An architect, educator, writer, and urban planner, he left California in 1968 to head up the architecture department at Massachusetts Institute of Technology, thinking that he was leaving for good. But as he puts it, "the California landscape was in my soul," so when he found himself with the opportunity to return to the University of California at Berkeley in 1978, he seized the opportunity. Although he had sold his original condo unit at the Sea Ranch in the interim, he knew that spending time there was key for him and his family. His return to Sea Ranch marked a new chapter in his life there, and since then he has designed numerous homes there and been on various committees that oversee both landscape and design direction and preservation. His search for the perfect place to build his own home took about five years. A large, rocky outcropping was the deciding factor that drew him to the site where the home he shares with his wife, Alice Wingwall, now sits. A duet of buildings bridged by a wooden deck, their home feels very much informed by the original Condominium 1 architecture that Donlyn helped create. I arrived early in the morning so I could catch the double-height living room being flooded with morning light. This room's built-in couch doubles as a daybed for a catnap in the sun when the mood hits, and a heart-shaped chair by Ron Arad was won at a benefit auction in Texas held by one of his former MLTW partners, Charles Moore. I asked what the story was behind the red-and-yellow color scheme in the house. It felt very Scandinavian to me, but apparently it was not completely planned, although red has always been Alice's signature color. There is even a vintage red-and-white Vuokko dress that Alice used to wear that now lives suspended at the top of the stairs in the bedroom, serving as art, sunshade, and privacy screen all at once. The smaller structure across the deck serves predominantly as Donlyn's office, but also houses the occasional guest. While I was there, he was working on one of the many plans for the Commons Landscape Committee, of which he is a key member. This takes up much of his time now and has produced ten detailed plans of the landscape along the sea ridge, defining their topographic characteristics—such as riparian streams, rock outcroppings, meadows, and hedgerows—and suggesting plans for the landscape's upkeep and maintenance. And it's Donlyn's voice and his observations of this land he loves that I hear as I take walks at Sea Ranch now. For all the attention the modern architecture gets here, it is the inextricable dance between it and this rugged California landscape that make the Sea Ranch so special. Donlyn Lyndon knows this intimately and is making sure it will be here for generations to come.

INTERIOR PORTRAITS

INTERIOR PORTRAITS

CATHY BAILEY & ROBIN PETRAVIC

—

SAUSALITO

Heath Ceramics is a California design institution. Known for its handcrafted ceramic dinnerware and tile, it was founded in 1948 by Edith and Brian Heath just north of the Golden Gate Bridge in the bayside town of Sausalito. Throughout the twentieth century, the Heaths built a legacy for creating beautifully designed ceramic pieces that were functional for everyday life. The first time I became aware of Heath was when I was in college. The Norton Simon Museum in Pasadena sat on my route to school so I drove by it every day. I deeply loved that building. It was a dark, Brutalist bruiser of a structure, but it wasn't until I finally stopped to get a closer look that I realized the dark brown "shingles" on the exterior were actually tile—Heath tile. Brilliant! Entering the twenty-first century, Heath's design legacy was secure but not that widely known outside of design circles. They were collected by museums and had won numerous awards and the factory was still producing in Sausalito, although the company may have seen better days.

Around this time, Cathy Bailey (b. 1967), an industrial designer, and Robin Petravic (b. 1968), a design engineer, had just moved to Sausalito from San Francisco. On a walk exploring their new hometown's shipyards, they stumbled across the Heath factory. This was a pivotal time for the couple. They had been working as design consultants for years and were looking for something new to sink their teeth into. Heath Ceramics, with its small, funky factory making beautiful things right in their backyard, inspired them. By 2003, they were the new owners of Heath and since then have carefully gone about reinvigorating the company while respecting its established legacy.

There is always a bit of trepidation when you hear that a company you love has been bought, and I have to admit I had a pang of anxiety when I heard news of the sale of Heath. But I hoped for the best and quietly watched as these new owners went to work. A few years later, I happened to be introduced to Cathy and Robin and as I got to know them I was also able to observe their work with Heath a bit more in depth. I have to say, the process has been a joy. I cannot imagine how two people could be more respectful of a company's legacy. They have slowly and carefully gone about streamlining the company on every level and have revitalized it to its former glory and then some. But beyond that, they are growing Heath into the future as more than a company—as a creative community.

When I asked to photograph their home, Cathy humbly described it as essentially an "old fisherman's shack with good bones." It was built in the late 1800s, so this description may have accurately described it at some point in history, but it definitely is not that now. They have renovated and remodeled in stages since they moved in 2002, and their home uniquely reflects their eclectic design aesthetic. Perched on the side of one of the many hills of Sausalito, the house overlooks rooftops and the boat-filled bay beyond. It is deceptively nondescript until you enter the front door. The entryway leads you into the heart of the main living area. On this floor the house is essentially open plan, so the sitting room spills into the dining room, which is open to the kitchen and the dark room used as a library to the rear of the house. A turquoise vintage wood stove with a Heath tile "hearth" at its back punctuates the dining area and beyond that sits their kitchen. Relatively small and efficient, its pale blue cabinets with contrasting hex tiles in two shades of blue offset a vintage copper stove that literally glows in the late afternoon light. The library, in contrast, is a deep shade of indigo and feels like a room where you could hang out and talk into the night. Toward the front of the house is what I call their modern Victorian sitting room. It is bold. Its contents are easily design classics from every era—a Marcel Breuer Wassily chair, an Alma Allen coffee table, and a vintage credenza—all surrounded by walls covered in Josef Frank Paradiset wallpaper in black. By far the thing in the room I most covet is a portrait they commissioned as homage to their beloved Newfoundland dogs Olive and Carlo (now deceased). A romantic, moonlit painting set at the seaside, it is endearing, funny, and a little strange in the best way possible. I want it.

One of my favorite things about Cathy and Robin's taste is that it is so unexpected. Their collections are very personal and quirky. Maybe I appreciate their taste so much because I know them a bit more than I do a lot of people whose homes I shoot, so some tchotchke on a shelf that I would normally overlook, for them I tend to wink and smile in acknowledgment because I understand its backstory. A small homage to Campari red (Cathy's cocktail of choice), an abstract Heath ceramic Newfoundland dog (their preferred breed), Robin's collection of ducks and both vintage and seconds of Heath pieces—these are their life loves and stories distilled into objects. Up the stairs, the top floor of the house sits directly under the sloped roofline and tightly fits a bathroom and two bedrooms, one for Cathy and Robin and the other for their son, Jasper. The "master" bedroom is not much larger than their son's and is as simple as the main floor is bold. A small window above the bed has the best view to the bay and to one side of the room is a small alcove that fits a vanity and Danish modern chair that used to belong to Edith Heath. There is something so right about Edith's chair sitting here woven into their life like a family heirloom. After all, their lives are intertwined through Heath Ceramics—each family's legacy—just as if they were related by blood.

INTERIOR PORTRAITS

SAM
MALOOF

RANCHO CUCAMONGA

S am Maloof (1916-2009) referred to himself simply as a "woodworker." He said he liked the word—it was honest. Clearly Sam also liked to understate things. Largely self-taught, he is considered one of the fathers of the American Studio Craft movement and is attributed with guiding it into the post-World War II era. He received numerous honors during his lifetime, including a MacArthur Fellowship (the only craftsman ever to receive one), and his work is coveted and collected by museums such as the Smithsonian and the Whitney Museum of American Art and collectors alike. Yet for all his accolades and truly beautiful work, I have always found myself more drawn to Maloof on a human level than I am by his work. I'm almost embarrassed to admit this because I have never met the man. But the first time I toured his home, I saw him through a window in his workshop. He was sitting there, laughing with the three guys that worked with him, and there was something that seemed so kind about him. I could sense his warm personality, even through the window. But my tour of his home left me feeling something else. I loved the house. Sam had built every part of it over the years he had lived there with his beloved wife and partner, Alfreda, and it was truly wonderful. It seemed a bit unplanned (he built on room after room as money allowed), yet it was undeniably a masterwork. But it felt like more than a house. It felt like a living symbol of the life and love of Sam and Alfreda. And if that were not complicated enough, Alfreda had passed away in 1998, so I also sensed a twinge of grief within its walls. Sam looked happy in his workshop that day (he had even remarried), but this home was still filled with Alfreda's collections of Native American artifacts and there were so many pictures of her that the home bordered on being a shrine. I walked away wondering how I could approach photographing a house imbued with such emotion. Can you capture that in a photograph?

It took seven years for me to return. I was brainstorming with a friend for the last few people to include in this book and Sam Maloof's name came up. Of course! He was perfect for it—an influential woodworking legend whose impact reached far beyond the borders of his native California. Yes! And it was time. Over the years, I had contemplated how the house had affected me so. It still left a lump in my throat. Sam had since passed away, so I hoped that the emotion I felt had shifted. I also realized that the heart of the home, where it felt the most authentic, was in the original footprint of the house that they had bought as newlyweds. So I made a loose plan to concentrate there.

The house defies any architectural typology that I know—it is wood shingled, with a verdant entry courtyard, and a front door that opens into an open plan living/dining/kitchen space. Inside it is rather dark, but sunlight drew me though to an exquisite wood and stained-glass door across the room. Through this door is another courtyard surrounded by workshops. A small cork-walled alcove sits in the light from the stained glass, with some of Alfreda's collection of kachina dolls and Native American pieces resting among books on the shelves. This open-plan part of the house is commonly referred to as the "original shoebox," and it is where I feel Sam and Alfreda's soul the most. It is a cozy space, made cheerier with vibrant colors (an acid-yellow couch with bright orange and bubblegum-pink walls!), Sam's woodworking flourishes, and the sweet details that are evidence of a dialogue between husband and wife. My favorite is in the room just off the kitchen. A sort of breakfast room / solarium with high ceilings and a row of clerestory windows, the room is paneled in wood and teeming with plants. Sam noticed Alfreda's difficulty watering all the hanging plants one day and devised an elaborate pulley system to lower them all easily, so she would never need a ladder to water again. I think it is daily kindnesses like this that show true love. The kitchen and dining area with its long table were central to both family and business life. Visitors and collectors would frequently come around since Sam and Alfreda's home was their showroom in the early days and many would be invited to share a meal. Apparently Alfreda made a mean casserole on the fly. The kitchen is simple and functional with chocolate-brown appliances that hark back to the 1970s. There is something so pleasing about the monochromatic room that I wonder why chrome is so popular now. As I continued to photograph the house, I could hear the sounds of furniture being made and wood being cut emanating from the workshops (Sam Maloof Woodworker is carried on by one of Sam's assistants), and it occurred to me how integral those sounds would have been when the Maloofs lived here. The sonic life of this house is rich, not just because of the woodshop but also the way your feet make a "chink, chink, chink" with every step on the brick floors. It was subtle and pleasantly melodious, like a woman's jewelry making a faint jingling as she walks. The master bedroom was in another wing of the house that had been added much later, but I felt Sam and Alfreda there too. Large photographs of them hung on the wall and Sam's signature piece, the Maloof rocking chair, sat at the foot of the bed. I suddenly realized I felt joyful this time around at the house. All those feelings of that first visit were gone, and Sam's warmth, which had drawn me through his workshop window, now flooded the house. I think it is because Sam's and Alfreda's souls are reunited.

INTERIOR PORTRAITS

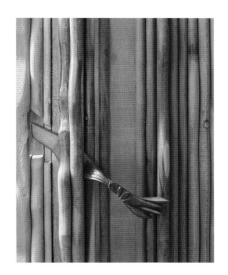

CHRISTINA KIM

———

LOS ANGELES

There is something very compelling about a person who is hard to figure out. Dark and light, hard and soft—everyone on the planet has degrees of each in his or her character. That is the beauty of the human race. But in my experience, there are few people who continually surprise me with every new layer I discover. Christina Kim (b. 1957) is just this type of enigmatic creature. I had been aware of her work for years before I met her. Her clothing line, Dosa, had been the favorite of a dear friend, so I associated her with delicate slips and flowing pants that had an indefinably old-world quality to them. Yet as I researched this book, looking for people who fit the bill of California creative mavericks, her name kept coming up—a maverick she definitely is.

Christina Kim is essentially an artist who has created a clothing line that is driven and inspired by her interest in art, ritual, and traditional world textile techniques and is a vehicle for evolving indigenous handcrafts with artisans she has collaborated with for years. Since the early 1990s she has been a proponent of running an environmentally sensitive company and stringently reviews how to remain ahead of the curve with current green thinking in a yearly review of the company's eco-aware agenda. At the time when I was photographing her loft in downtown Los Angeles, she was at an exciting crossroads in her life, putting the finishing touches on her final collection for Dosa while diving headlong into creating her company's next chapter and doing multiple artistic collaborations around the world—the first one being an installation with architect Peter Zumthor for the Venice Biennale. The space where she lives is just down the block from Dosa's headquarters and factory and is a jewel box of displays and living spaces all carefully arranged with objects from Christina's extensive collections and world travels.

The first time I entered 818, as Christina calls this full-floor space, I was a bit overwhelmed by the sheer beauty of it. Home, workshop, archive, showroom, creative laboratory, art space—it has served a multitude of purposes over the years. Christina has lived here part time for the past five years. The rest of the time she spends traveling the world. Located on the top floor of the 1924 Wurlitzer Building, she worked with architect Lindon Schultz to restore the building's original details of exposed brick and banks of curved windows along every wall looking out across the downtown Los Angeles skyline. It is hard to know where to look when you first enter. Look up and you'll notice delicate *papel picado* flags hanging from the ceiling, while in front of you is a sort of altar with a model of the Taj Mahal (made of Lego blocks). Looking back toward the double-entry doors, there is an antique Chinese opium bed tucked into the corner—a semi-concealed guest bedroom of sorts. Living spaces run around the perimeter of the loft, and low tables filled with objects arranged by color, type, project, or material run down the center. Because this space has been used as a showroom and for events, I quickly realized it was not the normal private home that I usually photograph and I needed Christina's help to decipher it. Her eye and hand are apparent in every single thing, but there are areas that are about her company and so somehow feel more public—like the long clothing rack holding every garment from her final collection and two tables filled with indigo and cream-colored objects that she assembled as an exhibit for the Textile Society of America. I asked where the active work areas were and she pointed to an old metal desk sitting among a remarkable collection of artist J.B. Blunk's wood and stone sculptures. The top of the desk is covered with ordered stacks of books, each pile being a future project that is percolating with the books she needs to research it further. I spent longer than usual photographing Christina's space because of the incredibly rich details that lie within it. Or that is what I told myself at the time. I realize now I was trying to understand her better. There is no question that I completely love the rigor and beauty of her space, but as I edited my images of it and even as I shot, I was most drawn to the slightly "undone" areas, like the corner where her overflow of books are piling up waiting to be shelved. Or the four years of old Filofax planners tucked on a shelf, with the story of each year of her life between its pages and her funny golf ball collection she began just because she had found a bunch of them at the site of her new home and she liked their shape and texture. These odd hiccups in such ordered beauty I found very refreshing and human—a step beyond the intoxicatingly rigorous beauty that Christina creates here and a glimpse of the more private version of herself that calls this space home.

Through observation, I came to see the three most personal rooms in the space as the kitchen, Christina's bathroom, and her "bedroom"—by which I mean her bed that is shrouded in vintage mosquito netting, making it a room within a room. The kitchen is easily my favorite space, perfectly functional and minimal. But beyond its design, the parts that drew me in most were again, the more personal bits—a little list of needed everyday objects she tacked to a shelf, the handmade giraffe her nephew made that sits on the dining table, and the delicate curtains, made from Dosa scrap fabric in an Indian appliqué technique that undulated and danced with the breeze from the open window. The Japanese mosquito-netting tent over her bed ended up being a source of some angst for me; there was something about that bed setup that was very private. It took me three days to peek underneath. But ultimately, I realized I liked the boundary it set—a layer too beautiful to peel away.

INTERIOR PORTRAITS

INTERIOR PORTRAITS

- wooden spoons
- 6" knife
- cheese grater
- measuring cup
- ~~knife~~
- toaster oven
- step ladder

CHARLES
MOORE

SEA RANCH

Architect, writer, educator, collaborator, world traveler, collector of folk art—to even scratch the surface of the eventful life of Charles Moore (1925-1993) in the short bit of writing here is a fool's errand. Thanks to his exuberant curiosity, he led four university architecture departments during his lifetime (University of California at Berkeley, Yale University, University of California at Los Angeles, and the University of Texas), founded seven architecture firms, wrote many books, and traveled the world insatiably until his death. In fact, on the day he unexpectedly passed away, he had his car packed to head from his home in Austin, Texas, to his condo in Sea Ranch, California. Although Moore was born in Michigan, California had been a constant in his life since childhood. During his time at Berkeley, the firm he had cofounded with college friends Donlyn Lyndon, William Turnbull Jr., and Richard Whitaker—MLTW, as they were known—was commissioned to be one of two architectural firms to create the original architecture that would inhabit the now historic experimental housing land development known as the Sea Ranch. Since it had been built, in 1965, Moore had kept a unit in the now landmarked Condominium 1 as a place of rest, meeting, and collaborative work and would return at least a couple times every year. I had no idea Moore's condo had been left relatively untouched by his family until I was deep in research on the Sea Ranch for this book. Donlyn Lyndon shared that Moore's family rented out his condo, so I decided what better place to stay as I photographed it and Donlyn's home for this book. Moore once said that the best way to understand a building is to be able to take a nap in it. I tend to agree with him but the opportunity to put this theory to practice is rare. I was not going to pass this chance up. It was December before I was able to return for the shoot and after months of drought in California, there was a big storm approaching as I arrived late in the afternoon. I barely had time to unload my car before the winds kicked up and the rain began to pound down. Without thinking, I left my things in a pile near the front door and curled up on the long window seat that looked out to the ocean and stared out the window until there was no daylight left.

Moore's home at Condominium 1—Unit 9—sits at its northernmost edge with unobstructed views to the north and west over a pocket bay to the Pacific. The exterior shape is simple yet substantial, inspired by the barns that originally dotted this coastal ranchland. And within it are all the major architectural moves that have made this building so influential since it was built. A glass box off the entry patio gives a glimpse of the ocean before you even step foot through the front door. Originally a solarium and workroom, it was converted to a bedroom in Moore's later years. Entering the front door leads you into the main living space with the stairs to the lofted second floor to the right. But it is only when you fully walk into the living area and look back that you get the full impact of the space, both architecturally and in terms of Moore's playful interior style. With the walls lined in Douglas fir and high ceilings, looking up reveals the iconic "four-poster" open bedroom suspended over part of the living room. Skylights shine light from above and I notice a ladder that leads to a loft high up near the ceiling. The house is filled with pieces from Moore's extensive folk art collection and world travels, architectural models, and even large reverse molds for plumbing pieces. They sit on every surface, hang from the walls, and even are balanced in the rafters. The intricate wall behind the wood-burning stove turns out to be part of a coffered ceiling originally intended for William Randolph Hearst's famous estate, Hearst Castle. Moore somehow procured it and playfully added some miniature horses to gallop out of it. Because I was staying in his condo, I had more time than I usually do to look closely at all the art, and my favorite ended up being a little architectural model of a barnlike structure. It was small and mounted on cardboard but its humbleness was endearing. Sadly, no one could tell me about its origins.

The second floor holds an open bedroom with a canvas tent hovering above the bed that you can lower down for privacy and a bathroom and closet, tucked down a few steps along the wall. I was completely powerless to resist my curiosity as to what was in the loft at the top of a ladder attached to the wall. I convinced myself it was important to get the aerial view from up there, so up I went with bare feet (which I do not recommend because *ouch!*—those round ladder rungs are a killer!). It was used for storage now, but Moore always had lots of people visiting and working with him when he was in residence, so it was definitely used as a sleeping loft at some point. I could see how it would be a favorite place to doze. My favorite spot ended up being right in the corner of the window seat, where I had beelined that first night in the storm. I constantly found myself nestling in there during my stay to watch the sunset, read, look at seabirds with the binoculars, eat dinner, soak up the sun—I even slept there a couple of nights. But mostly I just lay snuggled into the vibrant blue cushions and enjoyed the view and the sound of the surf below. By the end of my stay, its rhythmic sound felt like the heartbeat of this house.

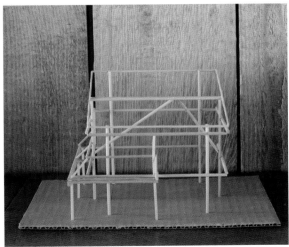

INTERIOR PORTRAITS

ALICE
WATERS

—

BERKELEY

t is virtually impossible to talk about Alice Waters (b. 1944) without using words that have been said many times before. Chef, restaurateur, author, food activist, and chief proponent of the Slow Food movement—there is no one who has influenced how people eat and think about food in America more than she has in the past fifty years. Her restaurant, Chez Panisse, has long been considered one of the best restaurants in the world and a training ground for some of the most important and influential chefs cooking today. To say her impact is far-reaching feels a bit understated. And yet, when a person becomes such an icon, there is a tendency for us not to think of them very deeply beyond that larger-than life-persona. I didn't realize this was true for me with Waters until I found myself photographing her garden for her landscape architect, Janet Hankinson. At the end of our shoot, Janet had to check on a few things inside the house for Alice, who was traveling, and so I came inside with her. Of course, I was curious—who wouldn't be? But I was completely caught off guard by the beautiful, humble simplicity of her home. I remember loving that an overgrown wisteria from the front yard had somehow snuck through the window and was allowed to grow into the living room. It seemed fitting somehow. It was late afternoon, the light was dark and shadowy, and I commented on how the light made me never want to leave the space. Janet said rather offhandedly that "Alice loves the light this way" and that she actually had an agreement with her neighbors to not trim their trees back too far so the light would be just like this. At that moment, as I heard that sentence, Alice Waters instantly became a different person to me. That little bit of information was so intriguing to me that my curiosity about who she really is beyond the big persona began to burn. When I began to work on this book, Alice Waters was immediately at the top of my list. She was born in New Jersey, but you cannot find a more iconic Californian whose influence reaches farther than hers. But also, I have to confess, I was just dying to be in her house again.

I arrived the morning of the shoot to a house that was rather more bustling than the empty one I had first experienced. Alice was working from home so that I could photograph her, and within the day she also had meetings, phone calls, visitors, and more. Yet even with five people milling around, the house was still remarkably peaceful, a classic Craftsman with all its dark woodwork and details restored to their original luster. I would call her interior style "Craftsman zen" for lack of a better way to put it. All the furniture is rather low to the ground and the colors are in dark shades of green, grays, and plums. The first room you enter from the front door is virtually devoid of furniture. With a small fireplace, a few seating pillows to one side, and a grand piano on the other, it is undoubtedly used for small performances on occasion. Through a small sitting room, you enter what is unsurprisingly the main room in the house—the kitchen and dining room. Dark green cabinets with glass fronts are filled with piles of glasses, bowls, and preserves, and the kitchen stove is surrounded by different salts, oils, and the most perfectly patinaed wooden utensils you could possibly have a need for. An oval dining table sits beyond the kitchen next to a brick wood oven that takes up virtually the entire wall, and a small table at the end of the room has a view out to her edible garden. This is where Alice likes to start her day, with a cup of tea and some reading. Off the kitchen is a room that I guess you could say is her office or workroom. The book-lined wall holds her library of cookbooks and books on food (her favorite being the 1825 French classic *The Physiology of Taste*), and it was here that she sequestered herself for the meetings she conducted throughout the day. Partway down a short hallway is the bathroom and at the end of hallway is Alice's bedroom, which is surprisingly small. During my visit, a vintage quilt in the palest shade of green covered the bed, which had a pillow that proclaimed, "Carpe Diem"—seize the day. The sitting room that I loved so much on my first visit had me in despair the day I shot. The light was way too dark to even think about taking a picture. But in the late afternoon, the light finally began to peek through the window. I must have made a kind of squeal of delight because both Alice and her assistant, Sam, looked in to see if I was okay. Slightly embarrassed, I said all was better than fine—the light was finally perfect! And with that, Alice playfully sauntered over and lay down on the couch just long enough for me to take two quick pictures of her faux napping before she headed back to work. After spending the day in her home, I began to hone in on what it was that I loved so much that first time I had visited. It was Alice's intense attention to detail. The color palette, the quality of light, and the assortment of her possessions— all are notably simple. Her home is not overfilled with things (in fact, it is rather sparse by American standards), but its contents are all carefully considered. She has made a home that contains only the things she most needs and loves and that are the most beautiful and meaningful to her, like a meal of favorite tastes. Hers is my favorite kind of home—a true and revealing portrait.

INTERIOR PORTRAITS

ACKNOWLEDGMENTS

These books are truly a labor of love. Although I photograph, write, concept, and research them largely by myself, no woman is an island. My work would be impossible without the support, knowledge, generosity, and help of many wonderful and very talented people and I am grateful to them all.

First and foremost, this book would not exist without the cooperation of the wonderful people it explores. Many thanks to you all for allowing me into your homes and lives: Alma Allen and Su Wu; Erin Lee Gafill, Tom Birmingham, Holly Fassett, Kirk Gafill, and the entire Fassett family; Kay Sekimachi; Roy McMakin and Mike Jacobs; Ray and Shelly Kappe; Madeleine Fitzpatrick and Evan Shively; Donlyn Lyndon and Alice Wingwall; Cathy Bailey, Robin Petravic, and their son, Jasper; Christina Kim; Alice Waters; Steve Weingarten; Kevin Keim of the Charles Moore Foundation; the Sam and Alfreda Maloof Foundation for Arts and Crafts, especially James Rawitsch and Linda Apodaca; and Vince Huth and the Robinson Jeffers Tor House Foundation.

A big thank-you to Rizzoli International Publications and Charles Miers for believing in this new Design Pilgrimage series and letting me run with it, and to my editor Dung Ngo, whose perspective I rely on, and Elizabeth Smith, for her copyediting magic. Thanks to Adam Brodsley and the team over at Volume Inc. for again making the book I imagined come to life through their design. To Dirk Hatch and everyone at Lightwaves Imaging for film processing and scanning throughout this project and indeed my entire career. To Lauren Matthews for jumping in at the last minute and helping with various odd, yet necessary tasks—you're a lifesaver! And, most importantly, thank you to artist and photographer Adam Thorman, who worked to make every single image in this book sing as only he can.

I am lucky to have a wonderful team of friends, and colleagues whose expertise and advice help me through making these books or who afforded introductions, recommendations, and encouragement at key points that moved the process along. I would really be lost without them. A very big thank-you to my agent Luke Janklow and his trusty assistant Claire Dippel at Janklow and Nesbit Associates for helping me navigate this next phase of my bookmaking life. Thanks to Fanny Singer, Janet Hankinson, Joe Kish, Gerard O'Brien, Maria Moyer, Karen John, George McCalman, Janet Pullen, Charles de Lisle, Christine Nielson, Roman Alonso, and Hugo Macdonald for the brainstorming sessions, ideas, advice, insights, and the ever-important intro email. To my dearest friends who put up with me through the roller coaster that making these books can be, your support, counsel, and belief in me and my work really do keep me going: Michele Janezic, Mariah Nielson, Mary Beth Phillips, Renée Zellweger, and Louisa Thomsen Brits.

A heartfelt thanks to my parents, Vicki Sykes and Cletus Williamson, who have supported my creative endeavors unwaveringly throughout my life and kept me planted in California soil until I was good and ripe. Thanks to my sister, Jennifer Williamson, who was my partner in crime and best playmate through all those trips to Yosemite and indeed my entire childhood and beyond. And to my uncle and aunt, Bob and Cyndi Connett, who listened when I needed it most and gave me a beautiful place in the redwoods to put the finishing touches on this book.

And, lastly, a deep and grateful thanks to California itself in every form that it takes: dream, reality, physical, metaphysical—you name it, I'm grateful for it. I plan on experiencing and exploring its wonders for the rest of my days.

First published in the United States of America in
2018 by Rizzoli International Publications, Inc.
300 Park Avenue South
New York, NY 10010
www.rizzoliusa.com
ISBN: 978-0-8478-6156-9

Library of Congress Control Number: 2017947952

Copyright ©2018 Rizzoli International

Photos & texts copyright ©2018 Leslie Williamson

Editors: Dung Ngo, Elizabeth Smith
Design: Volume Inc.

2018 2019 2020 2021 / 10 9 8 7 6 5 4 3 2 1

Printed in China